Reggie
Jackson:
Superstar
Dick O'Connor

SCHOLASTIC BOOK SERVICES
New York Toronto London Auckland Sydney Tokyo

Cover photo: Bruce Curtis

1st printing . . . . .April 1975
Printed in the U.S.A.

Reggie Jackson: Superstar

Author Dick O'Connor visits with Reggie Jackson before game as he gathers material for this book.

Chapter 1

When baseball fans voted for the 1974 American League All-Star team for the All-Star game, they knew there was a strong favorite in Reggie Jackson of the Oakland Athletics. But some of them didn't realize just how big a favorite Reggie was. Then the ballots were counted.

Reggie Jackson's selection to the All-Star team was the biggest landslide in the history of All-Star games. He polled 3,497,358 votes, the greatest number ever given to a player.

As one sportswriter pointed out, that was more votes than Abraham Lincoln got when he was elected President of the United States. (In fact, it was more votes than any of the first 26 presidents of the United States received.)

Reggie Jackson's total was also 1,000,000 more than the votes received by Hank Aaron of the Atlanta Braves, the leading vote getter in the National League. Rod Carew, the American League batting champion from Minnesota, was second in the American League voting, and his total was 2,402,968.

Was Reggie Jackson impressed by his popularity? He smiled slightly. "It's nice to know that people respect my ability," he said.

Reggie Jackson's ability is one of the most respected in baseball over the last 10 years. He is a 6-foot, 200-pounder with great all-around athletic skills. He has the speed, power, and grace of a super-athlete. Ever since he came up to the major leagues he has proved that he can hit, throw, run, and field as only few men can.

"He can beat you more ways than have been invented," is the way an opposing pitcher has described him. Naturally, Reggie Jackson has been one of the chief reasons the Oakland A's are the first team to win three straight World Series since the glory days of the New York Yankees in the early 1950's. (That once mighty team won *five* straight World Series — a record that may never be equaled again.)

It came as no surprise to anyone when Reggie was named the American League's Most Valuable Player in 1973. He had led the league in five ways: homers with 32, runs batted in, 117; runs scored, 99; game-winning hits, 18; and slugging percentage, with a hefty .531 for extra-base hits.

And along the way he received a tribute from Hall of Famer Ted Williams. "Reggie Jackson," said Williams, "is the most natural hitter I've ever seen."

Jackson began the 1974 season where he had left off the year before. He started with an explosive performance against the Texas Rangers. In the season opener, he had four hits including a homer, scored three runs, and stole a base to lead the A's to a 7-2 victory.

Two nights later he drove in seven runs with a pair of homers and a single as the A's whipped the Rangers 8-4. He got a standing ovation from the Texas fans as he went to right field in the ninth inning. "I tipped my cap to them because I appreciated their gesture," Jackson said.

After the game he spent almost half an hour signing autographs for Texans — young and old. "I signed scorecards, photos, hats, gloves, and everything. If they take the time to ask for my autograph, I have the time to give it to them," he said.

In a doubleheader April 14, he hit two homers and drove in four runs in the first game and had two more hits including a double in the second game.

Before the first home stand ended, Jackson collected 14 hits in 34 times at bat in nine games. He hit four home runs, four doubles, and drove in 12 runs.

A sportswriter asked Jackson what goals he set for the 1974 season. "I never set goals," Jackson said. "I have some ideas of what I want to do but I don't set goals. If I hit 25 homers and we win the pennant, it's a good year for me. If I hit 40 homers and we don't win, it isn't a good year."

Jackson's hot streak reached its peak against the Kansas City Royals on June 2 when he got three hits in three tries to boost his season average to .404 — best in all of baseball at that time.

For a while it appeared that Reggie Jackson might be the first player since Ted Williams, in 1941, to hit .400 for the season.

But Jackson's spectacular start did have a negative effect. "I couldn't concentrate on baseball," he said. "Everywhere I went there was someone who needed an interview or a picture. I wanted to play baseball...have fun...get my uniform dirty. You know, like a kid. But there was always someone who wanted something."

He was on the cover of *Time* Magazine at the height of the Watergate political scandals. "I'm the first person in quite a while to make the cover of *Time* for doing something good," he quipped.

Sports Illustrated also put him on the cover and called him baseball's "Superduperstar."

The extra demand on his time finally took its toll and Jackson went into a batting slump that chopped 100 points from his average. But with a sub-par second half of the season, Jackson still had a fine year. He was, as usual, the leader of the talented, brawling, championship Oakland A's.

He finished second to Dick Allen of the White Sox in home runs with 29, and hit a solid .289 with 93 runs batted in.

He missed the final two weeks of the season with a pulled hamstring muscle. That injury forced him into the role of designated hitter in the American League playoffs with the Baltimore Orioles. Jackson provided the big hit in the series with a double to put Oakland ahead 1-0 in the fourth and final game. It was the only hit the A's got in the game, a 2-1 victory over the Orioles that put them into the 1974 World Series for the third straight year.

Jackson got out of his mild batting slump in the World Series opener with a first inning homer that started the A's on the way to a 3-2 victory over the Los Angeles Dodgers. Reggie got two hits in Game Two despite a 3-2 Dodger victory. His hit highlighted a four-run sixth inning rally that beat the Dodgers 5-2 in the fourth game.

He saved the best for last, and this time it was a defensive gem in the fifth and final game. With the A's ahead 3-2 in the eighth inning, Bill Buckner hit a line drive to center field. The ball got by centerfielder Bill North but the alert Jackson was backing up his teammate. He scooped up the ball and fired a perfect throw to relay man Dick Green, who whipped the ball to third base in time to get Buckner and prevent what appeared to be an almost certain tying run.

The Dodgers were dead. And the A's were baseball champions of the world for the third straight time.

"This is the happiest day of my life," Reggie Jackson said with a sigh. "It's something I've dreamed of since I was a kid. And although I dreamed of it, I never thought it could ever happen. I sometimes wonder — how did I get here?"

Chapter 2

Reginald Martinez Jackson was born May 18, 1946, in Wyncote, Pa. a suburb of Philadelphia. His father, a better-than-average player in a black semi-pro baseball league, encouraged Reggie to play baseball.

"I guess it was because he never had a chance to play in the major leagues," Reggie says. "He wanted me to make it."

Reggie's father made it a very easy choice for his talented son to play baseball. "He told me if I didn't make the first team in baseball I would have to work in his tailor shop," Reggie recalls. "We lived in an apartment above it. That tailor shop was hot and steamy and full of hard, sweaty work.

"I didn't want to put in time in that shop so I really tried hard to make the baseball team. I first played baseball when I was five years old. It wasn't baseball...it was softball. I played first base but I really didn't care about that. All I wanted to do was bat."

Jackson was one of six children in the family and everyone played baseball. Reggie played Little League and was the smallest player on the team.

"When I was in the seventh grade I was only about 5-1 and weighed 100 pounds. But I could throw the ball hard. I mean real hard. That was another thing I liked to do besides bat. I always liked to throw the ball and it helped me develop a strong arm."

Reggie pitched some games; he threw hard, but he also was wild. "There was one game when I struck out 20 batters but I walked 14," he recalls.

In junior high school, Jackson played football and basketball in addition to baseball. He liked football the best.

"I thought I was best in football and I always dreamed of playing pro. But I really didn't think I would have a chance because I was so small."

His junior high school didn't have a very good team until Reggie arrived. "It wasn't just me. A whole bunch of good athletes came to the school at the same time. Before we came along there were a lot of rich kids in the neighborhood. They played but they weren't very good."

In basketball, Jackson averaged 18 points per game when he was in the ninth grade. He did some remarkable things for his size. "I could stuff the ball in the basket with both hands and I was only 5-8." Reggie was also the center on jump balls at the start of each quarter.

But baseball was where his talent showed the most. His first year at Cheltenham High School he hit .800. "That's right, .800. I had 16 hits in 20 times at bat. But I broke my left arm and couldn't play the whole season."

Reggie moved up to the varsity as a sophomore, and for the first time in many years, Cheltenham had a winning season.

"I had to play center field because they already had a first baseman," Reggie remembers. "I didn't like to play the outfield because there was so much standing around. I wanted to be doing something all the time."

Batting was still his first love. "I hated to swing at the ball and miss. There was one whole season when I don't think I swung at a pitch and missed. I mean for a whole season I don't think I missed once!"

Jackson also played his first football game as a sophomore and that, too, changed things at Cheltenham.

"We usually didn't win a game all season.

But there were a bunch of us dudes that made up our minds we were going to turn things around.

"The first game we played was against Dobbins High School. We always lost to them. But this time we beat them. I mean we really beat them. I scored four touchdowns in the first half and averaged about 11 yards per carry. We were so far ahead at the half, the coach wouldn't let me play in the second half. I think we won the game 44-13."

By the end of the season Jackson and his teammates were the talk of the league. Cheltenham won seven games and tied another. They lost only two.

In Jackson's senior year, Cheltenham won nine of 10 games. He played halfback on offense and safety on defense.

Reggie missed the final three games of the season because of an injury. He was playing defense and tried to tackle a big fullback. "I had a broken neck but no one really knew it until the day after the game. I was in a cast for three months and the doctors said I wouldn't ever be able to play ball again. At first they didn't think I would ever be able to walk again."

But Jackson made a remarkable recovery and when baseball season rolled around, he was back with the team again.

Reggie's final year of baseball earned him all-league and all-America recognition. He also was selected for the second time to play in a high school all-star game that matched the best players from Pennsylvania against the best from Florida.

"I was supposed to play in the game after my junior year but it was in Ft. Lauderdale, Florida. Because I was black they said I couldn't play. That's when I first found out about prejudice.

"The next year the game was in Pennsylvania and I was allowed to play. I finally got in as a pinch hitter in the last inning, but didn't get a hit. I made up my mind right then I was going to make it to the major leagues. I was going to show everyone I was a good baseball player and they couldn't keep me from playing."

Reggie still remembers his first baseball glove. "It was a Hutch. A Stan Musial model. I really liked that glove but I lost it off my bike one day. Then I got an Alex Carrasquel model. That was the best glove I ever had. I used that one all through high school and in the summer when I played on semi-pro teams."

Jackson's baseball career almost came to an end during practice for a summer game. "The best pitcher on our team didn't think I could get a hit off him. The very first pitch he threw was high and inside. I thought it was going to be a curve ball and break. But it didn't. It hit me right in the jaw."

Reggie's jaw was broken in five places and had to be wired back together. "But I couldn't stand having my mouth shut. I took some of the wires off so I could at least open my mouth."

Major league baseball scouts were interested in Jackson almost from the time he started playing the game.

"There was one guy who saw me play when I was only 11 years old. He told me I would make it to the major leagues some day. I guess that was the first time I really gave a thought to making a living playing baseball," Reggie says.

Jackson still wanted to play football too, and that was possible if he went to college. Although he was a good student in high school, he didn't have the money for college. He could get there only if he had an athletic scholarship. But for that the colleges would first have to notice him.

Chapter 3

Recognition was nothing new for Reggie Jackson. Baseball scouts had been watching him since he was 11 years old. They predicted future stardom. But Reggie wasn't sure he wanted to be a baseball player.

"I wanted to play football because you were doing things all the time. I wanted to be involved in the game. You know — running around and doing something. In baseball if I played the outfield there wasn't anything to do."

In the football department, college coaches were aware of Reggie's talent on the gridiron. They liked his quickness and speed.

"I got scholarship offers from 59 different colleges," Jackson said. "Notre Dame, Army, Michigan State, Temple, Princeton, Dartmouth, Oklahoma, and the Naval Academy were some of them.

"I even got one from Alabama. I guess they hadn't seen me play and didn't realize I was black." (This was back in the days before blacks played for colleges in the South.)

"Oklahoma knew I was black and they made a big thing of it. They told me I would be the first black football player at Oklahoma. I thought that would really be something."

Then Jackson heard about some of the other things he would have to do at Oklahoma. "They told me there was a curfew in Norman, Oklahoma, where the college is. I had to be off the streets by 10 o'clock at night. That was every night. I decided not to go to Oklahoma."

One of the few head coaches who paid a personal visit to Reggie was Frank Kush, the very successful coach at Arizona State University.

"I liked the idea of going to Arizona State because I knew they also had a very good baseball team," Reggie recalls. "Coach Kush convinced me to come to Arizona State. He told me about the campus and the good year-round weather. It sounded great to me."

Kush also promised Jackson that he would be one of the few athletes in Arizona State history who would be allowed to play both baseball and football. But there was a provision. "I had to have a 2.5 (B minus) grade-point average for my first semester. He said if I got it he would let me play baseball in the spring."

Jackson did it with flying colors. His grade-point average was 2.8, but Kush didn't really want Reggie to play baseball. He wanted Jackson for his football team and spring practice was very important to the fall success of the Sun Devils.

Reggie played on the freshman football team with many future pro stars like Curly Culp, Max Anderson, and Ben Hawkins.

"We played four games and we won them all," Reggie recalled. "We only had about three different plays. Whenever we needed yardage, Curly would just tell the quarterback to give the ball to me. Then Curly would say to me: 'Follow me!' Well, he weighed about 270 pounds and was awful strong. We always made the yardage. Sometimes I would grab his belt and he would pull me along behind him for a first down."

Reggie got to like football so much that he decided to give up baseball, for the first year at least. But a conversation with one of the other students in his dorm changed his mind.

"This guy bet me $5.00 I couldn't make the baseball team and still play football," Reggie grinned. "Well, I didn't have much money and that $5.00 was a big thing. I decided to give it a try."

Jackson showed up on the baseball diamond one afternoon after spring football practice and asked for a tryout.

"The coach let me swing at a few pitches and I hit the ball pretty good. Then he told me to lay down some bunts and run to first. I did it and he was timing me to see how fast I could run from home plate to first base."

The first time Jackson did it in an astonishing 3.3 seconds. Not even the fastest runners in the major leagues do it that fast.

"The coach couldn't believe the watch," Reggie said. "He told me to do it again because there was something wrong with his watch. This time I did it in 3.2."

The baseball coach still couldn't believe it, so he called over another coach to watch Jackson run.

When Jackson did it in 3.4, the coach was convinced there was nothing wrong with his watch. He also knew he had a potential baseball star in Jackson on his hands.

"From then on I played baseball," Jackson said. "And I collected my $5.00."

In his freshman year Reggie played the outfield. He hit .298 but had only two homers.

His fielding was spectacular. Often he threw out runners at home with great throws.

After the season, Jackson was offered a chance to play semi-pro baseball in Baltimore, Md. It was arranged by the varsity baseball coach at Arizona State, Bobby Winkles, who would later manage California in the American League and coach for the Oakland A's. Winkles was going to have Jackson playing for him at Arizona State the following year, and he wanted Reggie to get all the experience he could. He would not be paid in order to retain his college eligibility.

"He (Winkles) sent me to a man named Yost who had some connection with the Orioles. I showed up wearing my baseball spikes, my Arizona State shorts, and a ASU T-shirt. I didn't have a hat.

"Yost took a look at me and must have thought they had sent him the wrong person. He told me to hit. Well, the first three pitches I hit over the fence. Then I missed a few and he sent me to play the outfield." Reggie didn't realize it but he was getting a tryout with the team.

"When I got to right field, there was another guy there. We would take turns catching the ball and throwing it back in. I didn't find out until later that the other guy was the best outfielder on the team. It was a contest. I thought he was just trying out like I was."

Jackson made the team and had a good year. He played against many young players who later made it to the major leagues. Then he went back to Arizona State for his sophomore year and played defensive halfback on the football team that fall.

"I played on one side and Ben Hawkins was on the other. Curly Culp and Max Anderson also played. We had a good team and Travis Williams, who later played for Green Bay, was the star running back."

Reggie took part in spring football practice unless the baseball team had a game. Then he played baseball.

The 1966 baseball season was the one Jackson and everyone else had been waiting for. "I hit .327 and hit 15 home runs. That was a college record at the time. I also drove in 65 runs and threw out a lot of runners at the plate."

The homer everyone remembers was a blast at Phoenix Municipal Stadium where Arizona State played some of its games. Reggie hit a 480-foot drive that cleared the center-field fence. He was the first college player ever to hit a baseball that far in the park. In fact, Willie McCovey and Willie

Mays of the San Francisco Giants, who played in the same park every spring, never hit the ball that far.

Reggie made a clean sweep of honors at the end of the season. He was named to the all-conference team, to the NCAA District 7 all-star team, and also made the all-America team.

Jackson's final game in college was just what he hoped it would be. "All the scouts were there," as Reggie remembers it. "Not just the area scouts but the head guys — and the general managers were there too. They were the ones who decided how much bonus money to pay."

The first time at bat Reggie doubled. He also threw out a runner with a strong throw to the plate. The next time he impressed the crowd of 8,000, including the scouts, with his speed on a bunt single. Jackson capped the day by hitting a home run and got a standing ovation as he crossed the plate.

Then the wait began. Although he still had college eligibility left, he was also eligible for the pro baseball draft. Now he had to wait to see which club would select him.

He became the No. 1 pick of the Kansas City Athletics. That made him happy. "I had gotten to know their scout, Bob Zuk, and liked him," Reggie said.

The first offer from Kansas City was $50,000 — Jackson turned it down. "I wanted $100,000 because that's what they gave Rick Monday the year before and I felt I was just as good as he was."

Jackson decided to go back to Arizona State for his junior year and not sign a pro contract. Then he got a phone call from Charles O. Finley, the owner of the Kansas City ball club (later to be in Oakland). Finley invited Reggie and his father to come to see him.

"He offered me the same amount of money — $50,000 and I told him no. Finley was silent for a moment, then said he would cook breakfast for my father and me.

"Man, I really ate. I figured if he wouldn't give me the other $50,000 I wanted, I would eat up that much in food. I had about six pork chops, a dozen eggs, a loaf of toast, and everything that goes with it."

Finley then suggested he and Jackson go to Kansas City to see the baseball park. Reggie had never seen a major league baseball stadium before. "It was beautiful and I was impressed," Reggie said.

He met with Kansas City general manager Eddie Lopat and Finley. Finally, Finley offered Reggie $85,000, a new car, and enough money to complete his college education.

"I said, 'Give me the pen,' and I signed. They sent me to Lewiston, Idaho, in a rookie league and that was the start of my professional baseball career."

Chapter 4

Reggie's first pro baseball game in 1966 is still fuzzy in his mind. "It was in Lewiston, Idaho, and I was so excited just to put on the uniform I don't remember much else about it. I was doing what I always wanted to do — play baseball — and I was getting paid for it. I guess that's why I was so excited."

Jackson's professional debut, however, was sensational. He played 12 games for the Lewiston A's and drove in 11 runs.

Reggie will never forget one game during his brief stay in the Northwest League that summer of 1966. "Our home park wasn't very big. It was only 301 feet down the right-field line to the fence. The fence had a screen on top it. Beyond the fence there was a street and some houses on the other side of the street. My first home run as a professional baseball player landed on the roof of a house."

People who had been watching baseball in

Lewiston for many years couldn't remember ever seeing anyone hit the ball farther.

Reggie hit one other homer in his brief stay in the Northwest League. That was at Yakima, Washington. "The game was tied 2-2 in the 13th inning. The temperature was 29 degrees and it was almost snowing. I was getting cold and thought it would be a good time to get the game over with." The Yakima pitcher threw a fastball and Reggie hit a towering drive toward right field.

"The distance down the foul line was 350 feet. There was a light tower behind the fence and it was about 50 feet high. I hit the ball 30 feet higher than the light tower."

There never was any official estimate of how far the ball went because it disappeared into the dark of the night. Bill Posedel, a roving coach for the Kansas City A's, happened to be in Yakima and saw Jackson hit the homer. He estimated its distance at more than 500 feet. "It was the longest homer I ever saw and I saw quite a few," said Posedel, who had played pro baseball for more than 20 years.

Reggie hit only two homers for Lewiston. He remembers another hit very painfully. He was hit in the head by a pitch shortly after the long home run in Yakima.

When he was taken to the hospital, racial prejudice again reared its head. Jackson was refused a private room and assigned to a ward with other patients. But Posedel got things straightened out. "This is a very special baseball player. Mr. Finley, the owner of the Kansas City baseball team, wants him to have a private room," Posedel told the hospital officials.

"With a color TV," Reggie added.

He got his private room and the TV — and also a promotion to the A's Modesto farm team in the Class A California League.

There he joined some of the stars who later would win three straight world championships for the A's. Pitcher Rollie Fingers, catcher Dave Duncan, and outfielder Joe Rudi were already playing in Modesto when Jackson arrived.

"That was a big thrill moving up to another team," Jackson said. "Everything was so new to me but the important thing was that I was advancing toward the major leagues. And it was always a challenge because every time I moved up I was playing with and against better ballplayers.

"You wanted to be comfortable when you played but it was hard when you joined a new team. You knew someone from the big team was getting reports on your progress. You wondered how good you would be on the next level. Would you make it or get sent back to the team you came from?"

Jackson always came to the new team with a reputation as a budding superstar. "I was supposed to be the next Willie Mays or the next Mickey Mantle. People expected me to do this or that. I never seemed to get off to a good start anywhere because of that pressure. I wanted to show people I was as good as I was supposed to be and sometimes I tried too hard."

Reggie had been aware of the pressure to do well even in Little League days. "I was always the guy who had to drive in the runs and hit the homers. I had to win the game. I was always pressing...trying to hit the ball out of the park."

But at Modesto things were different. Duncan was on his way to setting a league home run record and Rudi was also having a great year. Reggie Jackson was just another player on a very good baseball team.

."Baseball was fun that year," he said. "The season was divided into two halves and we won the second half championship by 19 games. And that was for only a 60-game schedule."

It was a blazing first year for Jackson. In 56 games for Modesto, he hit .299 with 21 homers and 60 runs batted in. He also had six doubles and scored 50 runs. That gave him the following statistics for the full season which was divided between Lewiston and Modesto:

Games played: 68
Batting average: .297
Runs scored: 64
Runs batted in: 71
Home runs: 23
Slugging percentage: .602

If there was anything Jackson had to work on it was his frequent strikeouts and lack of experience in the outfield.

He went to the Arizona Instructional League that winter and worked. He played on the same team with Rick Monday, his former teammate at Arizona State University, and played against future major league stars including Bobby Bonds of the San Francisco Giants and New York Yankees and Ferguson Jenkins of the Chicago Cubs and Texas Rangers. John McNamara, who later would manage Jackson in Oakland, was in charge.

Reggie remembers two things about the winter of instruction. The first was that "it was the first time we ever wore the white shoes. Mr. Finley wanted to see how they looked before he had the major league team wear them."

The other thing Jackson remembers is the daily drills in the outfield. "McNamara would hit me 100 fly balls every day to improve my fielding. He hit 100 but I didn't catch that many."

Reggie finished the instructional league with a .240 average but cut down on his strike-outs and improved his fielding.

"It was tough to be a $100,000 bonus player," Jackson said. "There is the frustration of not playing well. And the pressure when you don't do as well as you think you should. If you never did well, they don't expect it. But have one good year and they expect you to do it every year.

"I struck out 81 times that first season. And I made every error you can make in the outfield. Heck, I didn't really know how to play the outfield."

The A's organization realized that Jackson had his faults, but they also saw a potential superstar. In 1967 they gave him a chance to show how good he really could be by promoting him to their Birmingham farm team in the Class AA Southern Association. If he could make it big in Birmingham, he would have a good shot at the major leagues.

Chapter 5

The Birmingham team trained in the wood-ed hills near Waycross, Ga. It was the first time Jackson had ever been in the deep South and he found very quickly that there would be trouble.

Jackson had just been released from military service after spending six weeks in basic training. He was declared physically unfit because of the back injury he had suffered in high school football. He was discharged just in time for spring training.

"I had just bought my first car. I went back to Baltimore and picked up my mother and my clothes and headed for Georgia."

Reggie remembers he was scared to death when he got to Waycross. "The first day I was there some people yelled racial insults at me, and told me to go home. And I couldn't eat in the same places as the other players. I decided right then that if I was going to play in the South, I was going to ask for more money."

Jackson's proposition to the A's was that he would sign for $700 per month and play for either Vancouver in the Pacific Coast League or Peninsula (Virginia) in the Eastern League. "But if they made me play in Birmingham, I told them I would have to be paid $1,000."

That really wasn't much of a raise. Jackson's salary his first year was $500 a month for a four-month season. Now he was asking $700 a month for a six-month season.

The A's offered him $600 a month to play in Birmingham. Jackson refused to sign.

"I'd had a good year in 1966. I hit almost a homer a game. I figured because of the circumstances, it would cost me $1,000 to live in Birmingham. I didn't sign until the last day of spring training. Mr. Finley called me personally and told me how much he wanted me to play in Birmingham.

"It was his home town and he wanted to win the championship. He was putting all the good young players in the farm system on that team so he could win. Joe Rudi, Dave Duncan, Rollie Fingers, Skip Lockwood, and Tony LaRussa were all on that team. I finally signed for $800."

The Birmingham team may have had the

largest number of bonus babies of any team in the history of the minor leagues.

"Lockwood had signed for a bonus of $100,000. LaRussa, the second baseman, got $90,000. Rudi got $50,000 and Duncan $60,000. Rollie Fingers got $40,000 and Don Buschorn $60,000. I got $80,000 and a kid named Johnson had signed for a $50,000 bonus."

When Jackson got to Birmingham for the start of the season he couldn't find an apartment to rent. He was the only black player on the team. He had to live in a hotel.

"Joe Rudi and his wife invited me over to their apartment to have dinner because I couldn't eat in most of the restaurants," Reggie recalls. "The manager of the apartment threatened to throw Rudi out if I kept coming over there for dinner." Reggie also ate at Rollie Fingers' place a few times but the same thing happened.

"I never had a date in Birmingham. There was a blonde girl who worked in the hotel where I stayed. She wanted to go out with me but I kept making excuses because I was scared of what would happen to us if we did go out together."

Reggie went to one restaurant in Birmingham where he thought he was welcome. "The waiter took my order and didn't say anything. I ordered a steak. When he brought the steak, he held it over his head and then dropped it on the table in front of me. Then he said, 'Don't you ever come in this restaurant again.' ''

There were problems on road trips too.

"We played a game in Knoxville, Tenn., and after the game Gil Blanco, one of our pitchers, and I went into a place to eat," Jackson said. "The waiter said he would serve Blanco but not me. Blanco almost wrecked the place he was so mad."

But the fans in Birmingham were good to Jackson. That helped him have an outstanding season.

In the middle of the year — 1967 — the call came from Kansas City. Reggie Jackson was going to the major leagues.

The call brought a curious reaction from Jackson. He didn't want to go. "I was scared. I was having a great year in Double A and wanted to stay and finish it. I was just a little boy. I didn't think I was ready to go up to the major leagues and play with the men."

But Reggie Jackson went.

"In the first major league game I played I was 0-for-3. Sam McDowell was pitching for the Cleveland Indians. He threw me a curve and I grounded out to shortstop."

Jackson got his first major league hit the next day against Orlando Pena. "He threw me a side-arm curve and I got a single. Stu Miller made me look very bad with his slow pitches. But I won a couple games with my bat and I went out every day and worked on my fielding."

After about a month, Jackson was hitting .178 and had struck out 35 times in 108 trips to the plate. The A's realized Jackson wasn't quite ready for the big leagues and sent him back to Birmingham.

Reggie was embarrassed about the demotion and didn't want to rejoin Birmingham. He went to Evansville, Ind., where Birmingham was playing and met with John McNamara, the manager.

"He told me the toughest thing I would ever have to do in my life was walk into that clubhouse, but that I had to do it."

Jackson did it. He played against Evansville that night and hit two triples to help Birmingham win 2-1. He quickly regained his stride and played well enough to be named Player of the Year in the minor leagues by *The Sporting News*.

For the season he hit .293 with 17 homers, 17 triples, and 26 doubles in 114 games. He drove in 58 runs and scored 80 runs. Reggie also stole 17 bases. "I could really run in those days," Jackson recalled.

After Birmingham defeated Albuquerque in the Dixie Series, Jackson was called back to Kansas City for the remainder of the 1967 season. This time he was ready.

"I hit my first major league home run off a pitcher named Jim Weaver and had a couple extra-base hits."

There was a high wall in right field in Kansas City which was tough for a left-hander to hit the ball over. The wall didn't bother Reggie for very long.

But there was turmoil in Kansas City. Manager Alvin Dark was fired after backing the players in a rebellion against owner Charles O. Finley. Finley, a colorful but controversial owner, insisted on meddling in his manager's work on the field.

The trouble was followed by talk that the A's would move to Oakland, California, for the 1968 season.

Before the season was over, Jackson was allowed to return to Arizona State University to resume his studies.

"I wasn't real excited about playing in the big leagues at the end of that 1967 season. I was looking forward to the time when I could make it and stay with the big league team for the whole season," he said.

Chapter 6

In 1968, Reggie Jackson made the major leagues to stay. The A's had been moved to Oakland, California, in a franchise switch.

"We didn't know much about it," Reggie said of the move. "We knew the team wasn't drawing too many fans in Kansas City so we weren't surprised when the team was moved. I didn't care where I played ball as long as it was in the major leagues. I was just a kid having a good time."

Reggie still felt the whole thing was a dream when he was told after spring training in Bradenton, Florida, that he would be the regular rightfielder for the Oakland A's.

"I really wanted to play baseball in the big leagues but I wanted to be ready. It was all new and fun. The fun went out of baseball later on and now it's a job."

The A's opened the 1968 home season in a game against the Baltimore Orioles at the sparkling new Oakland Coliseum. A capacity crowd of more than 47,000 turned out.

But the Orioles took some of the happiness out of the occasion by winning 4-1 on home runs by Brooks Robinson, Mark Belanger, and Boog Powell.

There were highlights for Jackson that first full season in the majors. And there were disappointments.

He struck out three times and went hitless in that first game in Oakland. But the next night he drew a walk to lead off the 13th inning and scored the winning run on a sacrifice fly by John Donaldson.

"I had a great year for a kid," Reggie said. "I would strike out a lot but also hit some homers. It seems there were some games when I would strike out three times and hit two taters." ("Taters" was Reggie's name for long home runs. "You know, a long tater," he explained.)

Before the year was over he would hit 29 home runs. Not bad for a 22-year-old kid.

"I made a lot of mistakes but it was fun. I was young and dumb but I learned a lot that year," he said.

Jackson really got rolling in July when he went on a home run spree. On July 7 he hit a pair of homers against the Detroit Tigers. A week later his three-run homer helped beat the Boston Red Sox. On July 19 he hit a three-run homer to beat Minnesota 4-3.

Three days later his homer helped Catfish Hunter beat Milwaukee 4-0, and four days afterward he drove in four runs with a homer and a double to beat Minnesota 8-7.

September 1 was a memorable day for Reggie as he slammed a 480-foot homer, the longest ever hit in Anaheim Stadium, to beat the Angels 5-2.

The big star of the 1968 baseball season was pitcher Denny McLain of the Detroit Tigers who won 31 games. But Jackson almost prevented McLain from reaching the magic 30-victory level. On September 14, McLain, with 29 victories, pitched against the A's in Detroit. With a national television audience watching, Jackson hit two homers and drove in three runs. But Detroit scored two runs in the ninth inning to win 5-4.

If there was a low point in the season for Jackson it was September 27 against the Minnesota Twins. In the first inning he faced Dave Boswell and struck out. Boswell got him on strikes again in the second inning. In the fourth inning Jackson batted against Boswell a third time and was called out on strikes.

Jim Roland, a left-hander, was pitching

when Jackson came to the plate in the sixth inning. Roland struck him out again.

In the eighth inning, Jackson got his final chance against a rookie named Bill Keller. Keller fooled Jackson with a curve ball for a called third strike.

Reggie Jackson had struck out five times in one game. He was stunned.

"Can you believe it?" he asked as he sat in front of his locker after the game. "We got 10 hits and I didn't get any of them. Their pitchers had only six strikeouts in the game and I was five of them."

But two days later Jackson hit his 29th homer of the season off Jim Merritt of the Twins to help the A's complete their best season in 16 years.

In 154 games that year, Jackson hit .250 with 74 runs batted in, 82 runs scored, 13 doubles, two triples, and 14 stolen bases. His fielding improved to the point where he was second in the league in assists by outfielders with 14.

His strikeout total was the second highest in the history of baseball to that date — 171 times. "I'm a free swinger," he said. "When you hit home runs, you also strike out. I can't change my style. That's the way I play. One of these days I'll cut down on the strikeouts and hit more home runs."

Chapter 7

The 1969 season got off to a slow start for Reggie Jackson. He didn't hit his first home run until the sixth game of the season when he smashed a 400-footer off Wally Bunker of the Kansas City Royals.

"I was a phenom," he explains. "Everybody expected me to hit homers and I was trying to do it. But I just couldn't get going."

His first visit to Yankee Stadium in New York in 1969 thrust him into national prominence. It was "The House that Ruth Built" — a baseball park where home runs were something special.

In the first of a three-game series, Reggie lashed a 420-foot drive into the right-field stands. The next night he hit another one even farther. The New York sportswriters, who had heard stories about the strong kid from the West Coast, decided Reggie Jackson was for real.

"It was a big thrill to hit the homers in Yankee Stadium," Jackson said. "They had those statues of the great Yankee players, Ruth and Gehrig, out there in center field. And now here I was...hitting home runs in the same stadium where they played.

"I could really thunder the ball in those days. I couldn't wait to get to the ball park. In batting practice I would see how far I could hit the ball." When Jackson took batting practice, players on the other teams stopped what they were doing to watch.

Jackson got some help with his hitting that year from Joe DiMaggio, one of the all-time stars of baseball. DiMaggio was an Oakland coach.

"He helped me with my hands. I was holding them too low and he got me to lift them so I could get a better swing at the ball," Reggie said.

DiMaggio also had another effect on the young star. "Just being around him helped me learn how a star should act. Joe DiMaggio has great poise. He knew how to act no matter where he was. He was a baseball star. He had done it all and he helped me handle the situations that came up that season," Jackson said.

On May 4, Jackson hit two home runs in a game against the Seattle Pilots and the writers started comparing Reggie with Babe Ruth. Every time Jackson hit a home run, the papers would indicate how far he was ahead of the record homer pace of Ruth in 1927 and Roger Maris in 1961.

Jackson became the subject of attention everywhere he played. And the home runs kept flying. "I really got hot in June. I was swinging well and everything was going great. I started to feel I could hit a home run every game."

And he almost did for one stretch in late June and early in July. He hit a homer to help beat the Kansas City Royals 3-2 on June 26. Another homer on June 29 was the clincher in a 6-5 triumph over the Chicago White Sox.

Jackson hit another in the next game — against the Seattle Pilots. The A's played Seattle again on July 2 — and it became a memorable game in Jackson's life.

"Marty Pattin was pitching for the Pilots. He's a tough pitcher, a little guy who never gives you a good pitch to hit," Jackson said.

But in the first inning Jackson got a good pitch to hit. He hammered it far into the right-field bleachers — more than 400 feet from the plate.

"When I got back to the bench, I told Lew Krausse, one of our pitchers, that I was going to hit some more homers in the game.

"He said, 'Some more? You mean more than one more?'"

Jackson nodded. "I mean some more home runs," he repeated.

Krausse began to wonder if Reggie was serious after Pattin struck him out in the third inning. But in the sixth inning Reggie connected again. This time it was a line drive over the center-field fence.

Seattle centerfielder Wayne Comer took only a few steps back and realized it was a waste of time to chase the ball. It landed in the center-field bleachers, more than 420 feet from where Jackson had hit it.

As he rounded third base, Reggie glanced up at the private box of club owner Charles O. Finley who was in town for the game. "I kind of waved at him as I stepped on the plate," Reggie said.

Diego Segui, who had been a teammate of Jackson's in 1968, was pitching for Seattle when Reggie came to bat for the final time in the eighth inning. Segui is noted for a sinker ball but the one he threw to Jackson didn't sink enough.

Jackson hit it over the center-field fence for his third homer of the game. He waved to Finley again as he crossed the plate and then went looking for Lew Krausse to say, "I told you I was going to do it."

Writers covering the game hurried over to Finley's box after the third homer to see if there might be a financial reward for Jackson. Finley had given pitcher Catfish Hunter a $5,000 bonus after he pitched a perfect game in 1968.

Would Jackson get a bonus? "No," Finley replied. "Reggie Jackson is paid to hit home runs."

By the All-Star break Jackson was the talk of the baseball world. He had 37 homers and had driven in 78 runs. The 37th homer came off George Brunet of the California Angels on July 20 — just two days before the All-Star game which was played in Washington, D.C.

Jackson was the leading vote getter in the American League, which entitled him to start in right field in the midsummer classic.

"I couldn't believe it," he said. "I would have been happy just to watch the game from the dugout...to sit there with the other big stars like Al Kaline, Carl Yastrzemski, Brooks Robinson, and Harmon Killebrew."

Jackson played the All Star game in a trance. He couldn't believe he had been selected to play. He went hitless in two trips to the plate.

"I was swamped by the press at the game. I didn't realize so many people had heard of me. I didn't have much chance to think about the game. They kept asking me if I thought I would break Babe Ruth's home run record. I told them I didn't know but that I would try my best."

After the All-Star game Jackson stopped getting as many good pitches as he had earlier in the season.

"The pitchers tried to get me to hit a bad pitch. If I didn't swing, I would get a walk. But they figured I wouldn't beat them with a home run," he said.

Jackson hit his 38th homer against Washington on July 25. He hit No. 39 the next day against the Senators in the ninth inning to tie the game 1-1. His 40th homer came July 29 against the New York Yankees.

At that point, with two months and 65 games to play, Jackson was more than two weeks ahead of the record home run pace of both Babe Ruth and Roger Maris. And it was then that Jackson stopped getting any pitches at all to hit.

The next day Yankee pitcher Mel Stottlemyre walked Jackson twice, once intentionally and the other thinly disguised as he threw four straight pitches out of the strike zone.

It got worse when the Boston Red Sox followed the Yankees into Oakland Coliseum. In the first game of a doubleheader, Jackson came to bat in the third inning with two outs and Ted Kubiak on second base. He was given an intentional walk by Lee Stange. He was walked again by Jim Lonborg in the seventh inning. With the A's ahead 9-7 in the eighth inning and first base open, Jackson was walked intentionally by Ron Kline.

Things got even worse for Jackson in the second game of the doubleheader. Sonny Siebert, the Boston starter, walked Jackson in the first, third, fifth, and seventh inning.

In sheer frustration, Jackson swung at a high outside pitch in the ninth inning and singled to left field. There was no way he could hit such a pitch for a home run. The frustration had begun to catch up with the 23-year-old Jackson.

"I couldn't handle it. It started to wear me down mentally. All I wanted to do that season was hit 50 home runs. I didn't care about Babe Ruth's record," he said.

In addition to his troubles on the field and not getting any good pitches to hit, Jackson was hounded by fans and writers off the field.

"I had to register in some hotels under my middle name — Martinez. Even that didn't help some places. It was unbelievable. The phone rang all night long. People were always knocking on the door. I don't know how they found out where I was but they did. I started rooming by myself because it wasn't fair to my roommate to be bothered by all those people."

The pressure finally caught up with Reggie in September. He was physically and mentally exhausted and was held out of the lineup for more than a week by manager Hank Bauer.

But he was back in the lineup for the final two weeks of the season. Reggie hit his 47th and final home run of the season at Seattle on September 30.

By then his chance of beating Babe Ruth's record was gone. But he still had a chance to win the home run title. He was tied with Harmon Killebrew of Minnesota. Each had 47 homers with two games to play. Killebrew hit a homer in each of the last two games to edge Jackson for the homer crown.

"Sure, I was disappointed," Jackson recalled. "But then I got to thinking that I had a pretty good year even if I didn't lead the league in home runs. I was happy because I proved I could play in the big leagues. I was proud of that. I was 23 years old and my future was still ahead of me."

It certainly was.

As a young collegian, Reggie discusses contract with Kansas City A's. Team later moved to Oakland, Calif.

Quick as a cat, Reggie takes a cut at the ball and almost in the same motion starts sprint to first base.

Action sequence shows Reggie's fielding ability and courage. He races for a line drive, crashes into the wall and tumbles to the ground, but holds onto ball.

Wide World

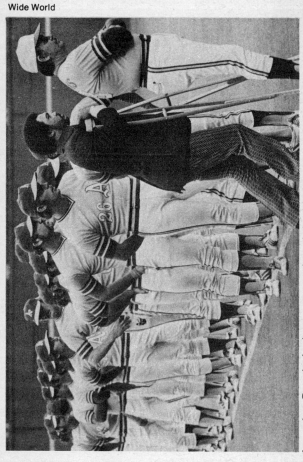

A somber Reggie Jackson on crutches. Injured near end of 1972 season, he missed World Series against Cincinnati but lined up with teammates for opening ceremony.

A soothing whirlpool bath eases Reggie's aches. Like many sprinters, his thigh muscles are easily injured.

*Reggie likes to start the day with a huge breakfast,
which often includes cereal, eggs, and pork chops.*

The owner of several cars, including antiques and drag-strip racers, Reggie checks a gleaming motor.

Reggie likes colorful clothes. He has hundreds of jackets, shirts, hats, and shoes for all occasions.

Reggie makes a point with then Vice President Ford, both honored by Touchdown Club in Columbus, O.

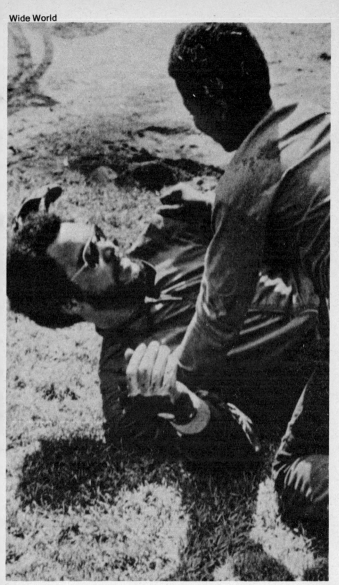

*Before dressing for a game, Reggie relaxes in a
friendly tussle with young Chris Burnell, A's bat boy.*

Chapter 8

If there was one game of the remarkable 1969 season that Reggie Jackson will never forget, it was the one played on a sunny summer afternoon in Boston on June 14. The Red Sox faced the Oakland A's, who were challenging for the lead in the American League West.

Jackson and Rico Petrocelli, the muscular Red Sox infielder, were battling at that time for the league lead in home runs.

"It was the best statistical game I have ever had," Reggie said of the contest. "I've had more important days, like the World Series, but from the standpoint of what I did in one game, that was the best."

And what did Jackson do ?

He came to bat in the first inning with two teammates on base. The score was 0-0. Lee Stange, a hard-throwing right-hander, was pitching for Boston.

Jackson lashed a long drive to right field that disappeared over the fence and the A's were ahead 3-0. The crowd of 22,395 fans buzzed at the strength of the young slugger from Oakland.

Blue Moon Odom was pitching for Oakland and he ran into trouble as the Red Sox got some runs and tied the score.

Jackson took care of that when he came to bat in the third inning. Stange was still the Boston pitcher. Bert Campaneris, the quick little A's shortstop, was on first base.

Reggie took a strike, a ball, then fouled off a pitch. The next one he lined against the wall in right-center field to send Campaneris scampering across the plate with the run that put Oakland ahead 4-3. The day was just beginning for Jackson and the A's.

He came to bat again in the fourth inning with Campaneris once more on first. Now Pat Jarvis, a tricky little right-hander, was pitching for the Red Sox.

Reggie made it easy for Campaneris to score and put Oakland ahead 7-5. He hit a line drive into the stands in right field, a rifle shot that left the park so fast the Red Sox outfielders didn't even have time to chase it.

Now the Red Sox fans were really excited. Who was this muscular youngster who had two homers, a double, and six runs batted in for his first three trips to the plate?

Boston manager Dick Williams, who later would have Jackson on his side in two World Series victories, sent in left-hander Dick Ellsworth to cool off the A's slugger. Reggie came to bat with the bases loaded against Ellsworth.

"This time I was thinking about driving in some runs," he recalls. "I didn't know how many I had so far but I knew I was having a good day."

But Ellsworth never gave him a chance to hit the ball. He drilled Jackson on the elbow with a fastball. Jackson just shrugged off the pain and trotted to first, getting credit for another run batted in. Now he had seven.

When Jackson came to bat in the seventh inning, Oakland led 14-7 and Ellsworth had long since headed for the showers. Sparky Lyle, a left-hander, was the pitcher, with a runner on second base.

Reggie smashed the first pitch to center field for a single. He hit the ball so sharply that the runner had to stop at third base. No matter that Reggie didn't get another RBI. There would be time for that.

In the eighth inning, he came to the plate for the final time. He got a standing ovation from the crowd. The bases were loaded and Lyle was still the pitcher.

"I got fooled on a curve ball," Reggie said. "I hit a little pop fly down the right-field line." It fell in for a double and all three runners scored. Jackson watched the ball fall out of reach of three Red Sox fielders as he trotted around first base. He just barely beat the throw to second base.

Manager Hank Bauer was waiting on the top step of the dugout when the inning ended. Jackson thought his manager was there to congratulate him for his sensational day. Instead Bauer, the ex-Marine, chewed out his young star for not hustling on the pop fly.

"You should have been on third base," Bauer growled.

"But we've scored 21 runs," Jackson replied.

Then Bauer told Jackson something he has never forgotten. "When you get the other team down, stomp on them," Bauer said. That was the way the Yankees did it when Bauer was a player.

The game ended a few minutes later with Oakland winning 21-7. For the day Jackson drove in 10 runs with two homers, two doubles, and a single.

"When I came into the clubhouse, my teammates gave me a standing ovation. That meant more to me than all those runs batted in," he said.

The next day the New England papers reported the details. They called it "The Boston Massacre." One writer said Oakland won because it scored three touchdowns and made all the extra points. How else, he wrote, could a team score 21 in a game?

"I saved all the clippings and the pictures," Jackson said. "The next day I hit two more homers off Sonny Siebert and went ahead in the home run race.

"Sure, I was excited about the big day and all the nice things people were saying about me. But the thing I remember the most was how much fun it was playing baseball."

Chapter 9

It didn't take long for the happiness of the 1969 season to be forgotten.

Specifically, it ended when Reggie Jackson got his contract for the 1970 season.

"I had had a great year in 1969," he said. "I figured I should get $1000 for each home run I had hit in 1969 — a total of $47,000. But I was sent a contract for $40,000. I didn't sign it. I sent it back and then sent it back a second time. I wasn't fooling around. I felt I was worth $47,000 and wasn't going to change my mind."

Neither was club owner Charles O. Finley. The holdout continued and when the Oakland A's assembled at their spring training camp in Mesa, Arizona, Reggie Jackson was not present.

He was in nearby Tempe, Arizona, where he had become a partner in a real estate firm. The days turned into weeks and Jackson still refused to sign his contract unless he got $47,000.

For five weeks Jackson sold real estate while the A's prepared for the 1970 season. Finally, 10 days before the start of the regular season, Finley offered to compromise.

"He said he would give me $45,000 and pay the rent on an apartment for me in Oakland during the season," said Reggie.

"I signed the contract and started looking for an apartment." As it turned out, Finley would have been wiser to have given Jackson a contract calling for $47,000.

Reggie found an apartment, a lavish spread of rooms overlooking Lake Merritt, in Oakland. It was just across the lake from the luxury apartment that Finley himself rented when he was in Oakland.

When Finley found out how much the rent was on Reggie's apartment, he tried to change the agreement.

"I told him if I couldn't keep the apartment, with him paying the rent, I would quit baseball and go home," Jackson said.

Finley agreed and Reggie played the 1970 season. But the lack of spring training and the hassle over the contract took its toll both physically and mentally. Jackson was not in good shape to open the season and his mental attitude was not right for the entire year.

"I get off to a slow start every year," Reggie said. "But that year I just wasn't ready. I had worked out during my holdout but that's not like hitting against good pitchers. I just wasn't ready when the season opened."

Jackson struck out five times in one game in the first week of the season and shortly afterward, for the first time in his baseball career, Reggie was benched. He was now at the low point of his career, and when he got another chance to play, he still failed to produce.

Manager John McNamara, after a talk with Finley, decided to bench Jackson whenever a left-handed pitcher faced the A's. This didn't help either. Jackson not only wasn't hitting home runs. He wasn't even hitting singles.

Finley then made a surprising announcement. "If Jackson doesn't start hitting, we may have to send him to the minor leagues. If there is one individual who is hurting this team, it's Reggie Jackson."

Reggie was angry when he was told of his possible demotion to the A's farm team in Des Moines, Iowa. "I'll tell you one thing," he said at the time. "I won't go. If he would have signed me earlier, I would have been ready to play."

Shortly afterward, McNamara decided to

bench Jackson against right-handed pitchers too. His batting average was barely above .200.

McNamara called Jackson into his office for a private meeting that lasted more than an hour. He asked Jackson to go to Des Moines for a while to get himself in shape.

"I told him I was a major league baseball player," Jackson said. "I know I can play for someone. People say if I don't hit, the A's can't win. Well, when you're sitting on the bench, it takes an awful long bat to hit."

Jackson stayed with the A's and his batting average went up a little.

"If I couldn't help the team with my bat, I tried to help in other ways," he said. "I stole 26 bases, the most I have ever stolen in a season. And I think I did a good job in the outfield."

Jackson got back into the regular lineup in August but was benched again early in September.

On Sept. 5, the A's played the Kansas City Royals at Oakland Coliseum. Finley was making one of his infrequent appearances at a game in Oakland. With Oakland ahead in the eighth inning and the bases loaded, Jackson was sent in as a pinch hitter.

"I wanted to hit a home run," he said. And he did hit one — the first grand slam of his major league career. Jackson slowly trotted around the bases. When he got to the plate, he stopped, looked up at Finley's private box behind home plate, and made an angry gesture.

Two days later, in Chicago, Reggie paid for his disrespect. Finley summoned him to a meeting which also included manager John McNamara and the coaching staff. Finley asked Jackson why he made the impolite gesture.

"Because I hate the way you treat me and the way you treat people," Reggie explained.

But Finley got his way and Jackson signed a statement in which he apologized to Finley, the coaches, his teammates, and the fans.

The rest of the season went quickly. The A's were out of pennant contention and Reggie finished the year with a .237 batting average, only 23 home runs, and 66 runs batted in.

He batted only 426 times, more than 100 fewer than he had the year before. And he led the American League in strikeouts for the third year in a row with 135. Reggie Jackson was happy when the season finally ended. He headed for Puerto Rico to play winter baseball.

And that's where he started the long comeback which would make him the best baseball player in the American League.

Chapter 10

After the 1970 season many things changed for the Oakland A's.

The biggest change was a new manager — tough Dick Williams who had led the Boston Red Sox to the American League pennant in 1968.

Owner Charles O. Finley of the A's was tired of not winning the pennant. He figured Williams was the man to change all that.

Reggie Jackson wanted to change some things too. He wanted to forget the salary hassle and disappointments that cropped up in 1970. For Reggie, it was simply a poor season. Strangely, he began to strike out a lot. Frequently he was benched.

"I played winter ball in Puerto Rico. I decided I would be ready when the 1971 season started. I realized how much it had hurt me, and the team, when I wasn't ready in 1970," he said.

During the off season Jackson had asked to be traded, but the request was denied by Finley.

"I have no hard feelings about that," said Reggie. "Be a good Christian and forget. What happened in 1970 was just as much my fault and probably more. I need him to play ball. And he needs me to play for him."

Jackson tore apart the Caribbean League. He played almost every game in the short winter season and hit 20 homers, breaking the league record set many, many years before by Orlando Cepeda's father.

"The manager of the team was Frank Robinson, a man who I had great respect for. He helped me straighten myself out." (Later, Frank Robinson would be appointed manager of the Cleveland Indians — major league baseball's first black manager.)

"I got off to a bad start and he told me the only way I could go was up. He showed me how to play winning baseball. When things went wrong he didn't get mad. He just tried harder. And he didn't make mistakes. I learned from him."

Dick Williams paid a visit to Jackson in Puerto Rico. "He was interested in me. No other manager took the time to do that," Jackson recalls. "He told me I was going to play every game for him no matter what I was hitting. There wouldn't be any more platooning (left-hand hitting outfielders against right-handed pitchers and vice versa). He said he was looking forward to having me play for him."

That was logical. Williams was the manager of the Boston Red Sox the day Reggie drove in 10 runs against them.

Jackson had heard stories about what kind of manager Williams was.

"I had heard bad things about him...that he didn't stick up for his players when things got tough. When he came down to Puerto Rico he seemed too happy. But I figured I would wait and see for myself what kind of manager he was."

Jackson signed his contract and was present when the A's opened spring training in Mesa, Arizona. He did everything right. He hit 10 home runs. He hustled on every hit. He played well in the field. He earned the respect of his teammates.

Jackson slid hard to break up double plays and was always looking for an extra base. Singles became doubles and doubles were turned into triples.

"The one thing I was concentrating on was cutting down my strikeouts," Jackson said. "I struck out only 14 times in 66 times at bat that spring. That was about once every five times at bat." The year before Jackson had struck out more than once in every three times at bat.

When spring training was over, Jackson made some predictions. "I feel I have it in me to hit 50 home runs. I think I can lead this team to a pennant. I feel it is in my blood to be the Most Valuable Player."

Jackson gave Frank Robinson and Dick Williams the credit for his new attitude. "Frank told me that if I could just hit the ball more often I would hit .300. Dick Williams was a leader. He had been a winner. He taught us how to be winners."

Despite the good spring and his new attitude, Jackson got off to a slow start. He was in a slump when Williams called him in for a two-hour talk on April 26 in Anaheim.

"He said I was going to stay in the lineup even if I was hitting .105," said Reggie. "He said I had to hit if Oakland was going to win. That gave me confidence and also a challenge."

In the month of May, Jackson hit .360. And for the rest of the season he continued to hit.

The A's made a runaway of the pennant race almost from the start. With Catfish Hunter, Vida Blue, and Chuck Dobson pitching the victories, and Jackson, Joe Rudi, Sal Bando, Mike Epstein, and Tommy Davis doing the hitting, they went into first place in the Western Division of the American League on April 20 and never trailed again.

"Dick Williams made the difference," Jackson said. "We had most of the same players we had the year before but he showed us how to win."

There were ups and downs for Reggie. On May 19 he hit a two-run homer to help Vida Blue beat Milwaukee 3-0. He brought a dramatic end to a May 25 game against Chicago with a 13th inning homer as Oakland won 7-5.

His best series of the season came in August against Boston, much to the delight of Dick Williams who had been fired by the Red Sox in 1969. On Aug. 21 Jackson had three hits including a pair of homers and drove in three runs to beat Boston 4-1. The next day, in the second game of a doubleheader, he hit a ninth inning homer to give the A's a 2-1 victory over Sonny Siebert.

"Baseball was fun again," Jackson said. "I guess that was because we were winning. And everyone was contributing. It wasn't just the pitchers or the hitters. We were winning as a team."

By Sept. 1, Oakland was 17 games ahead of Kansas City. It was just a matter of time until the A's clinched the pennant. On Sept. 11, against the Minnesota Twins, Reggie reduced the magic number to two with a two-run 10th inning homer that gave the A's a 5-3 victory.

Two days later, the A's beat Chicago 3-2 in the first game of a doubleheader and Kansas City lost to the California Angels. The A's were the Western Division champs.

The celebration was quiet. Dick Williams was tossed in the shower with all his clothes on. There was some shouting but no champagne. The A's decided to wait until after the American League playoffs with Baltimore to have their champagne.

As it turned out, they should have had it when they clinched the division title. The bottles were never opened.

"We were no match for the Orioles in the playoffs," Reggie said. "They had been there before and had the experience of playing in big games. We were just as good as the Orioles but we were afraid of them. They had the big reputation and all those good pitchers. We lost the playoffs in three straight because they had the Robinsons — Brooks and Frank."

Ironically, this was the same Frank Robinson who taught Jackson a winning attitude in the Puerto Rican Winter League.

When the last playoff game was over the dejected A's — all but one of them — trudged into the clubhouse. Jackson sat alone on the dugout steps. He was there for almost 30 minutes after the game, alone with his thoughts.

"That was the loneliest and saddest day of my life. I wondered if maybe we would never win the big games," he said. Finally, Reggie got up and took the slow walk to the clubhouse. His eyes were red from the tears of defeat.

"I knew we would be back the next year. And this time we would be ready. A player has to be in a big series once before he can win."

As usual, Reggie Jackson was right.

Chapter 11

The young Oakland A's came into the 1972 season a good choice to win the American League pennant. True, they had suffered a great disappointment in losing to the Baltimore Orioles in the league playoff the year before. But now Joe Rudi, Rollie Fingers, Sal Bando, Catfish Hunter, Vida Blue, and Reggie Jackson were sure nothing would keep them from their first flag.

Nothing did stop the Oakland A's. But Reggie Jackson was stopped.

Reggie had sprinter speed of 9.6 for the 100-yard dash. He was a remarkable athlete with impressive muscles. He had 17-inch biceps, 27-inch thighs, and he had the arms of a blacksmith and the shoulders of a fullback.

But sprinters with thick thighs have to be very careful about muscle pulls and hamstring tears. Reggie Jackson was no exception.

Several times during the season he had to play at reduced speed.

"It was terribly frustrating," he recalls. "I wanted to help more but there were days I could hardly run."

He still contributed plenty, however, as the A's ran away with the Western Division of the American League and met the Detroit Tigers in the playoffs.

Reggie had hit 25 homers for the year. His rifle arm had prevented many a base runner from scoring. But fate wasn't on his side. The Oakland-Detroit playoff was a bitter battle that went down to the last out of the decisive fifth game before the A's won it. But Reggie Jackson's heart wasn't entirely in the celebration that followed, because he knew he wasn't going to be in the World Series.

Playing it to the hilt was the only way Reggie Jackson knew how to play baseball and in the fifth game of the playoffs it cost him. He stole home to score a vital run but was injured in a collision at the plate with Tiger catcher Bill Freehan. He never recovered in time to play against the Cincinnati Reds in the World Series.

"All my life I dreamed of playing in the Series and now I couldn't do it. It was one of the saddest times of my life," Reggie said.

Fans in both Cincinnati and Oakland made things a little brighter for Jackson. He was introduced before each game and hobbled onto the field to a tremendous ovation.

The A's beat the Reds in a thrilling seven-game Series and this time Jackson was right in the middle of the celebration after the final out.

Then, a year later, it finally happened. The day Reggie Jackson had waited for all his life arrived. The impossible dream had come true. He was playing in the World Series.

It had been a great season in 1973 for Reggie, as he looked back at it. "It hadn't started on a happy note, though," he recalls. What he meant was that in spring training, owner Charles O. Finley had traded away the A's catcher, Dave Duncan. Duncan had been a close friend of Reggie's. When Jackson heard of the trade he was furious. He tore his uniform off and refused to take the field for practice. It was an hour before his teammates got him to change his mind.

Reggie was now one of the team leaders. Pitchers Vida Blue and John Odom got off to a poor start and were feeling low; it was Reggie Jackson who talked to them and got their spirits up.

When manager Dick Williams benched Joe Rudi it was Reggie who came to Rudi's defense. Rudi was soon back in the lineup.

Although Jackson pulled a hamstring muscle and missed some September games, it was his clutch hitting that sparked the A's to the pennant.

For the season he got 158 hits and scored 99 runs. His batting average was just a few points under .300 but he blasted 32 homers and had 286 total bases. He also stole 22 bases. It was Reggie's finest year since 1969 and the fans knew it. All baseball knew it when he was named the American League's MVP.

Now it was Oct. 13, 1973, at Oakland Coliseum. The New York Mets, the National League champions, were being introduced. There was polite applause for the visitors from the crowd of 46,021 fans. Wayne Garrett...Felix Millan...Willie Mays...and finally a big hand for manager Yogi Berra.

Now it was time for the Oakland fans to salute their team. The first was Bert Campaneris and then Joe Rudi. Next came Sal Bando. Even before the next name could be announced the cheering began.

"Playing right field and batting fourth, No. 9...Reggie Jackson." He got a standing ovation as he trotted out and took his place along the third-base line with his teammates.

"I really didn't believe I had finally made it to the World Series. After the year before, when I was hurt, I just didn't believe it," he said.

Reality came to Jackson moments later when he sprinted out to center field for the start of the game. "I guess some of the other players on our team weren't nervous because they had played in the World Series the year before against Cincinnati. But this was the first one for me. And I was nervous."

In the second inning Reggie got his first turn at bat. The pitcher for the Mets was Jon Matlack, a tall right-hander with a good fastball.

"I was too anxious. He threw me a good pitch and I grounded out to shortstop," Reggie said of his first swing in a World Series.

He came up again in the third inning and popped out to New York first baseman John Milner. That was the third out after the A's had taken the lead with two runs off Matlack. Jackson drew a walk in the sixth inning and then grounded out again in the eighth.

Now it was the ninth inning and the A's still led 2-1. Oakland pitcher Rollie Fingers walked pinch hitter Ron Hodges to put the tying run on first base.

Jim Beauchamp, another pinch hitter, lined out to second base and now Wayne Garrett

77

was the batter. He hit a towering fly toward right field. Jackson drifted over a few steps, reached up, and made his familiar one-handed catch. The A's were one game ahead in the World Series.

But Reggie Jackson wasn't happy. "I hope I'm not the scapegoat in this thing. I didn't help the team," he said in disappointment.

Actually he had made a big contribution to the victory. With a Met runner on first base and a run already across in the fourth inning, Jackson made a running catch of Jerry Grote's bid for an extra-base hit.

Game Two matched Vida Blue of the A's and Jerry Koosman of the Mets in a battle of left-handers. This was the day Jackson would turn on the batting power.

He singled in the fifth inning but Gene Tenace hit into a double play to end the inning. He doubled off Met relief ace Tug Mc-Graw with two outs in the seventh but Tenace struck out.

New York led 6-4 going into the ninth inning. Pinch hitter Deron Johnson led off for the A's with a double and, after the next two batters were retired, Sal Bando drew a walk.

"It was up to me," Reggie said. "I just wanted to get a pitch I could handle."

He got one and lined a single to right field to score Johnson. Tenace followed with a single to tie the score and send the game into extra innings.

The Mets went ahead with four runs in their half of the 12th inning, three of them on errors by substitute second baseman Mike Andrews.

Reggie came to bat again in the 12th inning and McGraw was still pitching. He hit a line drive to center field that got by Willie Mays for a triple. Jesus Alou got him home with a single but it wasn't enough as the Mets evened the Series with a 10-7 victory.

The big story started to unfold shortly after the game in the office of manager Dick Williams. Club owner Charles O. Finley, embarrassed by the defeat, summoned second baseman Mike Andrews to a meeting. Andrews had played poorly in the field. Andrews, on orders from Finley, signed a medical statement that he was unable to play in the remainder of the Series. Andrews left the team.

The story of the meeting leaked out to the other players on the charter flight to New York for the third game of the Series.

Said Jackson: "The team was close to mutiny when they found out what had happened to Andrews. Nobody wants to see a teammate fired that way in the middle of a World Series."

The next day, at the A's workout at Shea

Stadium in New York, many of the players had Andrews' number — 17 — taped on their sleeves in memory of their departed teammate.

Once Game Three began, the turmoil was forgotten. The Mets jumped off to a 2-0 lead against Catfish Hunter in the first inning, and with Tom Seaver pitching, it seemed insurmountable. But the A's got a run in the sixth inning and another in the eighth to tie the game. They won in the 11th inning on a single by Bert Campaneris.

Jackson was hitless in five trips to the plate. Seaver struck him out three times. Reggie had nothing but praise for the Met pitching ace. "He's the best pitcher in baseball. Even people in China have heard of him. Blind people come to games just to hear him pitch. He can really pop that catcher's glove."

The fourth game was a runaway for the Mets. Rusty Staub hit two homers and drove in five runs in a 6-1 victory.

Jackson had a single in four trips to the plate.

"We just didn't have a chance to concentrate on playing baseball," Reggie said. "After the Andrews thing, Dick Williams told us he was quitting as manager after the Series was over — whether we won or lost."

The slump for Jackson and the A's continued again in Game Five as Jerry Koosman and Tug McGraw combined to pitch a three-hit shutout. Now the Mets needed only one more victory to win the world championship.

"Our backs are to the wall," Jackson said on the flight back to Oakland. "But we've been there before. We play our best baseball when we have to win." And in Game Six, the real Reggie Jackson stood up to be counted.

In the first five games he had left 17 teammates on base, hardly what is expected of a slugger who drove in 117 runs during the regular season.

With a capacity crowd of 49,333 fans looking on at Oakland Coliseum, Reggie Jackson almost single-handedly destroyed the Mets' dream of a world championship.

He came up for the first time in the first inning with Joe Rudi on first. Jackson lined a double to left-center field and Rudi rambled home with the first run of the game.

In the third inning, Jackson delivered again. This time Sal Bando was on first base. "I was just trying to meet the ball, hit it good," Jackson said afterward. "That's all you do against a pitcher like Tom Seaver. Just meet the ball."

He doubled to right-center field and Bando

scored to make it 2-0. And Jackson wasn't through yet.

The Mets scored a run off Catfish Hunter to cut the A's lead to 2-1. Jackson hit a line drive to center field that got past Don Hahn and rolled to the fence. He was credited with a single, his third hit of the day, and Hahn was charged with a two-base error.

Jesus Alou's sacrifice fly got Jackson home with the final run for Oakland. Not a bad performance in a crucial game. Jackson had driven in two of the Oakland runs and scored the other.

Seaver paid him a fine compliment after the game. "I threw Jackson a fastball in the first inning and he hit it to left field for a double. Then I threw him a good sinker ball in the third and he hit that to right field for another double. He's some hitter."

And now it was the final game of the World Series. This would be for everything — the money, the diamond rings which signify a world championship, and the prestige.

For the third time in the Series, it was the same match-up of pitchers — Ken Holtzman for the A's and Jon Matlack for the Mets. Holtzman had won the Series opener 2-1, and Matlack won Game Four, 6-1.

The first two innings were scoreless. Jackson came to bat in the first inning with Sal Bando on first base and grounded out to end the inning.

"We knew something was going to happen and we wanted to make it happen," Reggie said.

It happened in the third inning. Holtzman started the rally with a double and trotted home with the first run when Bert Campaneris followed with a home run just beyond the left-field fence.

The A's were ahead 2-0. Joe Rudi followed with a single but Sal Bando popped out.

Now it was Jackson's turn again. He picked out a fastball to his liking and lined it for a home run into the right-field bleachers to make it 4-0 for Oakland.

"I never enjoyed anything so much in my life," Reggie said. "Every step of the way around the bases was great." When he came to home plate, he leaped high in the air and came down with both feet on the plate.

The rest of the game was fairly easy for the A's. Holtzman got relief help from Darold Knowles and Rollie Fingers to nail down a 5-2 victory.

The dressing room was a wild place as the A's celebrated their second straight world title. Right in the middle was Reggie Jackson, smoking a big cigar and sipping the victory champagne.

"What can I say?" he asked. "It's the greatest day of my life. The greatest. This is the best team in baseball. We proved it by coming back to win."

Then he left the celebration and went through the tunnel to the Mets' dressing room. He congratulated Met manager Yogi Berra and some of his players for an excellent Series.

When he got back to his own dressing room, he was told he had been selected the Most Valuable Player in the Series. The honor also won him a new automobile from *Sport* Magazine. "Great, great...just great," he said and came close to breaking into tears.

For the Series, Jackson had nine hits in 29 trips to the plate for a .310 batting average. He hit a home run, a triple, and three doubles. Of the 21 runs Oakland scored in the Series, Jackson drove in six of them and scored three times.

After the Series, Jackson revealed why he perhaps didn't play even better. "A couple weeks before the end of the season, I'd received a phone call from Mr. Finley. He told me to hustle over to the ball park immediately for a meeting. I sensed an urgency in his voice. I'd soon find out what was up."

"When I got to the ball park, there were three FBI men there and they had a letter they wanted to show me. The general tone of the letter was a threat on my life. It said that if I played in the American League playoff, it would be the last thing I would ever do." The threatening letter, signed by "The Weatherman," was addressed to Monte Moore, the A's radio announcer.

From that day on, Jackson was protected by the FBI and also by his own personal bodyguard — Tony Del Rio, a 290-pounder who stands 6-5.

Reggie said he tried not to let the threat affect his play in the playoffs and World Series. "I didn't take it all that seriously and I don't think it affected my play. But still, I had it on my mind. You don't dismiss anything like that easily."

After talking with Finley and the FBI men, Jackson decided to take part in the playoffs and World Series. "I felt if I got knocked off, I'd rather have it happen on the baseball field."

Fortunately, Reggie Jackson didn't get knocked off on the baseball field or anywhere else.

Chapter 12

Just exactly who is Reggie Jackson? Is he baseball's next superstar, as many people claim? Is he destined to go down in baseball history with outfielders like Joe DiMaggio, Mickey Mantle, Ted Williams, and Willie Mays? Or will he always be on the brink of super-greatness, plagued by injuries?

Fans ask other questions. Is he a brash, arrogant man who brawls with his teammates and anyone else he disagrees with? Is it true that he is a bright young man who goes out of his way to help others?

"I guess you can say almost all of those things are true," says A's third baseman, Sal Bando. Bando is captain of the team and has known Reggie since their college days together at Arizona State.

"Reggie has a world of ability," says Bando. "He has had his problems and he can be tough to get along with. But he is a warm, likable human being.

The 29-year-old Reggie lives in a beautiful and expensive apartment high in the hills that overlook Oakland. It is tastefully furnished and next to his huge, showpiece brass bed is a red telephone.

"Only three people have the number to that phone," says Reggie. It has to be that way or it would never stop ringing. He is constantly besieged by people wanting him for this or that — for testimonials for their products, for TV and radio appearances, for interviews, for speeches at banquets.

In the morning when he gets up, he makes his first decision. What shall he wear? In his three large closets he has more than 100 pairs of slacks and 100 shirts. He has 50 sports jackets and leather jackets, and can choose from among more than a dozen hats and caps of varied style and color.

His first stop each morning is a tiny restaurant called Lois the Pie Queen. He likes it because its customers are a wide range of both blacks and whites, and Reggie gets along with them all. Reggie waves to many of them whom he knows on sight, slaps a few backs, or chuckles a joke to a waitress. Then he sits down to orange juice, pork chops and rice, scrambled eggs, biscuits, and milk.

A white friend will frequently join him. "There are 200 million people in this country," Reggie points out, "and 180 million of them are white. That's why many of my social friends are white, both men and women."

As often as not, Reggie's next stop will be at an auto shop in San Leandro, a town near Oakland. Reggie owns five racing and show cars. He has puttered around with cars ever since he was a kid, and years ago he vowed cars would be his greatest pleasure if he could afford them.

"I can really relax at the shop," says Reggie. "It's like an amusement park for me. So much to see while the mechanics are working on different kinds of racing cars, or restoring old models. I also like to wash the cars myself. It gives me pleasure."

Two of Reggie's are a 1940 Chevy and a beautiful 1927 yellow Ford roadster. The roadster happens to hold the world record for quarter-mile drag racing. Reggie often spins this one himself, on unoffical runs. He also likes to climb aboard a souped-up motorcycle and let it out once in a while. Naturally, the Oakland A's management doesn't like the idea.

"I guess I could get a Rolls Royce now, but

then I wouldn't have anything to buy when I get to be 45 years old," he said with a grin.

Behind the scenes, Reggie Jackson is a sensitive and kind man. He has been known to pay doctor bills for young people who need help. He has also set up a home for delinquent boys in Tempe, Arizona, near his winter home.

He remembers the hardships of his own youth, and many of his friends'. He recalls how so many of his young friends got in trouble, and he wants to do his bit in helping kids who are desperately in need of aid. Reggie has also given financial aid to Indian tribes in Arizona.

"If you have money, why not spread it around," he smiles. With his quarter of a million dollar salary he makes each year from baseball and his outside interests, he can do so. He also has additional income from an Arizona land development company, in partnership with a former college friend.

According to some reports, Reggie's interest in the land company makes him a multi-millionaire. But he never thinks of retiring from baseball early. "I'm having too much fun," he says. "That's what baseball is — pure fun."

But baseball isn't the only thing he knows. He speaks easily, with a brilliant vocabulary.

He can talk about anything — politics, religion, soul music, or big business.

But once he arrives at the ball park, Jackson lives and breathes baseball. A few years ago he could tell you the uniform number of every player in the major leagues. With expansion teams, he hasn't kept up as he once did.

Before the game, Jackson talks with the fans. He is cordial and seems genuinely interested in their problems or views on baseball. "They are the people who are paying my salary," he says. "I feel I owe them something."

Jackson has had problems with some of his teammates. When you play with the Oakland A's, you always know where you stand. If a teammate doesn't like you, he lets you know.

Reggie had a well-publicized fight with teammate Bill North in Detroit midway in the 1974 season. So intense was the brawl that catcher Ray Fosse, acting as peacemaker, suffered a neck injury that kept him out for almost two months. Jackson won't talk about the fight. He has since made up with North who plays next to him in the outfield.

Three years ago there was a clubhouse fight with teammate Mike Epstein. They became closer friends afterward than they were before.

"Reggie can be immature," one of his teammates said. And Jackson will readily admit he still has some growing up to do.

He was married when he was 22 but divorced less than four years later.

He is usually the first player the sportswriters flock around after a tough game. Jackson always has something to say — win or lose.

"But I don't like to waste my time with people who ask the same questions all the time," Jackson said. "I like a challenge from a writer, just like from a pitcher."

If a reporter asks a dumb question, Jackson lets him know it. "You're wasting my time," Jackson will answer.

However, should the same question be asked by a youngster in the parking lot after a game, Jackson might spend 15 minutes giving an answer.

Jackson enjoys his status as a baseball star. "There are times," he says, "when it would be nice to be treated just like everyone else. But there are times when I do like to get special treatment. But mostly, all I really ask is to be treated with respect."

And respect — a lot of it — is what Reggie Jackson has earned, and gets.